DANGEROUS DRUGS

# OXYCODONE

### JACKIE F. STANMYRE

Cavendish
Square
New York

Published in 2016 by Cavendish Square Publishing, LLC
243 5th Avenue, Suite 136, New York, NY 10016

Copyright © 2016 by Cavendish Square Publishing, LLC

First Edition

Library of Congress Cataloging-in-Publication Data

Stanmyre, Jackie.
Oxycodone / Jackie Friedman Stanmyre.
pages cm. — (Dangerous drugs)
Includes bibliographical references and index.
ISBN 978-1-50260-558-0 (hardcover) ISBN 978-1-50260-559-7 (ebook)
1. Oxycodone. 2. Oxycodone abuse. 3. Drug abuse. I. Title.

RM666.O76S73 2016
615.7'822—dc23

2015004883

Editorial Director: David McNamara
Editor: Fletcher Doyle
Copy Editor: Rebecca Rohan
Art Director: Jeff Talbot
Designer: Stephanie Flecha
Senior Production Manager: Jennifer Ryder-Talbot
Production Editor: Renni Johnson
Photo Research: J8 Media

The photographs in this book are used by permission and through the courtesy of: Universal Images Group/Getty Images, cover, 1; Education Images/UIG/Getty Images, 4; Everett Historical/Shutterstock.com, 7; AP Photo/U.S. Marine Corps, 8; CentralITAlliance/iStockphoto.com, 12; Mukhina Viktoriia/Shutterstock.com, 15; Adrian Weinbrecht/Cultura/Getty Images, 18; Meletios/Shutterstock.com, 20; Steve Grayson/WireImage/Getty Images, 22; Juniart/Shutterstock.com, 25; Selimaksan/iStockphoto.com, 28; Ximagination/iStockphoto.com, 30; The Santa Fe New Mexican, Luis Sanchez Saturno /AP Images, 33; Diego Cervo/Shutterstock.com, 34; Casarsa/E+/Getty Images, 37; ktaylorg/iStockphoto.com, 41; John Greim/LightRocket/Getty Images, 42; John Ewing/Portland Press Herald/Getty Images, 45; Bikeriderlondon/Shutterstock.com, 46; James Devaney/FilmMagic/Getty Images, 49; Photodisc/Getty Images, 53; Jon Bradley/The Image Bank/Getty Images, 54; Tracy Whiteside/Shutterstock.com, 57.

Printed in the United States of America

# Contents

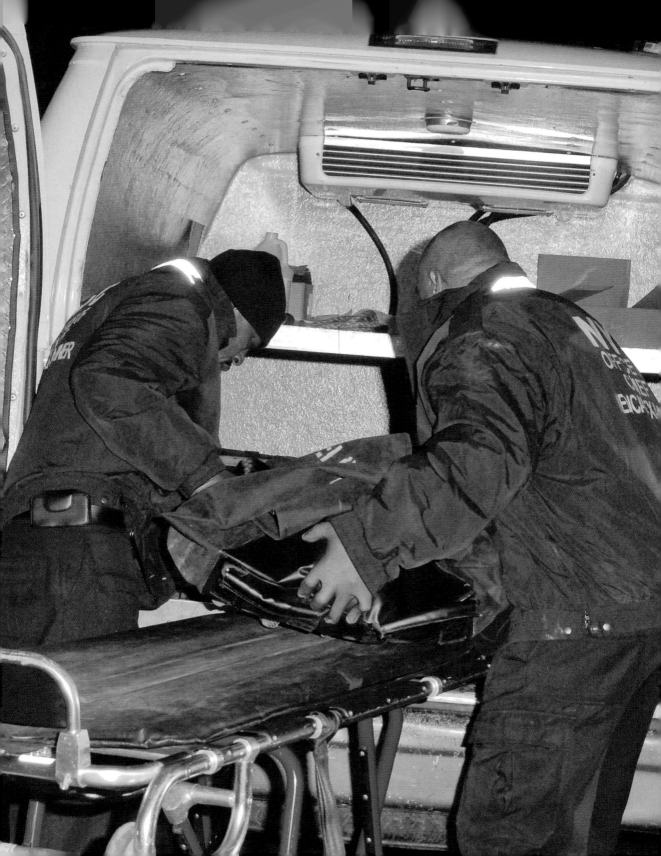

# CHAPTER ONE

# Inflicting Pain

**H**EATH LEDGER'S MASSEUSE AND housekeeper found his lifeless body near his bed on January 22, 2008. They did not find illegal drugs: there was no **heroin**, no cocaine. There was not even any alcohol. But the tragic death of one of the country's finest film actors was, in fact, related to extreme drug abuse.

When the **toxicology** report came back two weeks after Ledger's death, it showed there was a cocktail of drugs found in his system—all prescription drugs that any doctor may prescribe. One of the most potent and increasingly deadly drugs in his system was oxycodone, a medication often given to patients for pain management following a surgery or for long-term relief for individuals suffering from cancer or arthritis.

The body of Heath Ledger is loaded into an ambulance. The actor died as a result of abusing drugs, including oxycodone.

But in the past twenty years, oxycodone has become one of the most abused drugs in the country, leading to addiction and death. One in eight people who experimented with drugs for recreation report that a pain reliever was the first drug they ever abused, second only to marijuana.

"This is terrible and I'm in shock," a close friend of Ledger's told UsMagazine.com. "But to tell you the truth … we saw it coming. Things were very dark. His one joy was [his daughter] Matilda. Everything else was misery for him. Unfortunately, he was too late in getting help."

## Search for a Substitute

Oxycodone is an **opioid**, which is a synthetic or semisynthetic substance that is made to have an effect much like opium. An opiate contains, or is made from, opium or the opium poppy.

Opium has been around for centuries, and it is made from flowers called poppies. In the eighteenth century, Britain used opium produced in India to pay for goods made in China, such as tea and silk. India is one of the world's largest growers of opium poppies. With opium addiction climbing in China, the emperor seized all the opium and had it burned, setting off what was called the Opium Wars.

Asians who came to the United States to work brought opium with them, and addiction spread. Scientists began to search for a safer form of the drug that they could use for its medicinal qualities. A man named Friedrich Wilhelm Serturner developed a drug he named morphine early in the

6

Opium dens became a problem in Asia. The drug, which is used to make opioids, came to the US from Asia and was known to cause addiction.

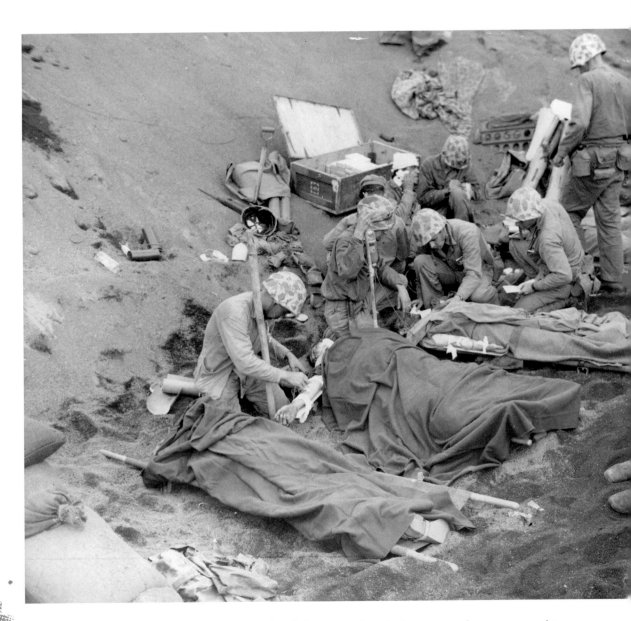

Morphine, which is made of the same chemicals as oxycodone, was used to treat soldiers in World War II.

nineteenth century, and by mid-century it was being used as a painkiller and as a cure for opium addiction.

Morphine was commonly used to treat wounded soldiers, and it soon became clear this drug was also highly addictive. Scientists again tried to find a drug that could kill pain without being addictive, and they developed heroin. Heroin was sold by Bayer Corporation in Germany, and it was later found to be highly addictive.

When heroin was banned in the United States, German scientists developed oxycodone, which was thought to be a non-addictive substitute for opium, heroin, and morphine. Doctors have been prescribing oxycodone since 1917. Originally, its main use was to treat pain experienced by patients who had recently had operations. It also was seen as useful for cancer-related pain or other severe medical pain. Unfortunately, researchers and doctors had no idea the problems that would follow.

Oxycodone is in the opioid drug family. Other drugs in this family include **hydrocodone** (Vicodin), fentanyl, **methadone**, and codeine. All of these are used for relieving severe pain, and all have the potential to be abused.

In the 1960s, the United Nations Office on Drugs and Crime classified oxycodone as a "dangerous drug." At this time it became considered a Schedule II **Narcotic** by the Drug Enforcement Agency (DEA). This definition indicates that oxycodone has a high potential for abuse; oxycodone has an accepted medical use in the United States; and oxycodone abuse can lead to severe psychological or physical addiction.

# Overdoses in Overdrive

Doctors knew oxycodone was helpful in relieving pain but also saw that it could be dangerous. Still, it stayed on the market and eventually got even more publicity. It grew more popular—and more deadly after the time-release OxyContin was approved in 1995. In 1996, oxycodone was linked to forty-nine deaths in the United States. In 2008, oxycodone and hydrocodone misuse led to almost fifteen thousand deaths in this country, or more than forty deaths from overdose *per day*. Prescription drugs, both legal and illegal, are one of the leading causes of accidental death in the country.

Those numbers indicate an explosion in oxycodone overdoses over the past several decades. The Centers for Disease Control and Prevention (CDC) reported that twelve million Americans abused prescription painkillers in 2010. In 2009, abuse of oxycodone led to almost 176,000 emergency room visits. Oxycodone combined with other opioids or painkillers led to 1.2 million hospitalizations that year. In 2004, there were about 627,000. This means that the amount of people who landed in the hospital because they were abusing painkillers nearly doubled in just five years.

There are other drugs that have oxycodone as a main ingredient. Among them are Percodan, Combunox, Roxiprin, Roxicodone, Endocet, Endodan, and Percocet, which is oxycodone combined with acetaminophen, the pain-relieving

10

agent in Tylenol. Oxycodone is a chemical found in many drugs, whereas OxyContin refers to a specific formulation of the oxycodone drug.

These drug names are the official ones used by doctors or hospitals. Some "street" names for OxyContin include: Cotton, Pills, Kickers, OxyCotton, Ox, OCs, Orange County, Os, Oxys, Killers, Beans, or Rushbo. Percocet may also be known as Paulas, Roxis, Blue Dynamite, Percs, Roxicotten, and 512s.

There is a false notion that drugs prescribed by a doctor, such as oxycodone, OxyContin, or Percocet, must be safe. The pain-healing effects of the drugs also lead to a "high" feeling similar to that obtained from using illegal drugs. Some users have reported feeling a head rush or increased pleasure over basic activities, like listening to music. One oxycodone user posted on a blog that he remembers "not having a care in the world." But the high never lasts. And the need to find more of the drug becomes consuming.

Those who abuse drugs are known for developing a single, solitary care in their lives: getting more drugs. They will begin to experiment with a variety of substances, as they try to achieve that same high. They will start to experience **withdrawal** symptoms, which can make them violently ill unless they replace the drugs in their system. Their bodies adapt to the drugs, then need them. They may experience

Withdrawal symptoms that start when someone stops using oxycodone can feel like an extremely bad flu.

insomnia, diarrhea, vomiting, cold flashes with goose bumps, and involuntary leg movements.

To support their habit, many addicts turn to stealing money from their families or strangers, or selling family valuables. Often, people who are addicted to a drug find they are spending hours every day making sure they have enough of it.

## Cheaper Alternative

The high cost of oxycodone pills has been shown to lead drug users to seeking out a cheaper high. Known for being less expensive and leading to similar feelings and effects on the mind and body is a drug that may make you a little more cautious: heroin. As oxycodone use has exploded across the country, heroin use has become an **epidemic**. Heroin is also in the opioid family, meaning it makes a person's body feel similar to how it feels when it is on oxycodone.

"Because readily available prescription pills have become a gateway drug, heroin is finding its way into the world of people who never imagined that they would ever confront this terrible substance," said the chairman of the Governor's Council on Alcoholism and Drug Abuse in New Jersey. "This is hardly the traditional path to heroin abuse, and that is one of the things that makes the present situation so troubling."

Oxycodone—and heroin—abuse are not confined to poor, urban streets. They're found in the suburbs and in wealthier neighborhoods, with the strength to get their claws into almost anyone.

# Suburban Drug Use

Close your eyes and picture a drug addict. What sorts of images come to mind? Someone in poverty, living in the inner city, maybe even homeless? Well, oxycodone is telling you to think again. As prescription pill use has soared, drug abuse has begun to take over the suburbs. In many of these places, heroin has become an even bigger drug problem than pills.

In 2012, 156,000 people tried heroin for the first time. A study in Charlotte, NC, found the majority of heroin users were from the five most affluent neighborhoods—those full of lawyers, nurses, police officers, and ministers.

"Folks are looking for that better high," a police chief in Minnesota said. "Lots of them started with prescription drugs. When that didn't do it, they would start crushing them. And when that didn't work, they turned to more of the street drugs."

People who have abused prescription painkillers are more likely to experiment with heroin.

One of the reasons oxycodone abuse is so prevalent is the easy access. People who have been prescribed oxycodone sometimes have extra pills in their medicine cabinet. Fifty-three percent of people who abused pain relievers got them for free from a relative or friend, according to the Substance Abuse and Mental Health Services Administration (SAMHSA). Meanwhile, 21 percent got them from a doctor, and almost 15 percent bought or stole them from a relative or friend.

The journal *Academic Emergency Medicine* did a study on the number of prescriptions written for narcotic painkillers. It found that between 2001 and 2010, emergency departments in the United States increased the number of prescriptions they wrote for these painkillers by 49 percent. The greatest increase was in oxycodone prescriptions for patients leaving the hospital and still in need of pain relief.

# CHAPTER TWO

# Low Tolerance

**O**XYCODONE ABUSE MAY START WITH a doctor's prescription and a trip to the pharmacy. People may question why such an addictive drug would be prescribed. However, there are strong medical reasons for taking the drug.

A person's central nervous system (CNS) sends signals throughout the body using neurons. Neurotransmitters transport chemical and electrical signals across synapses, which are the gaps between neurons. At the end of a neuron—there are billions of them in your body—are dendrites that receive signals and allow them to enter the neuron. There are different neurotransmitters and **receptors** for different functions. Neurotransmitters dampen or stimulate activity in the neurons they target.

Your body naturally produces and transmits opioid-like neurotransmitters called endorphin and enkephalin,

17

Our brains release chemicals during all types of activities. Exercising produces endorphins.

which are received by opioid receptors. These receptors let your brain know if you're feeling pain and can block it. Endorphins, for example, are released with exercise. They work with receptors to reduce your perception of pain, and they produce positive feelings.

Oxycodone stimulates your opioid receptors, changing how much pain you feel and how you respond emotionally. Oxycodone can also be used to suppress coughing or slow breathing. The most common results are pain relief and feelings of euphoria, or extreme happiness. It does work as a painkiller and can allow a person who is injured to function.

## Changing Signals

But oxycodone, even when prescribed by a doctor, should not to be taken for more than a few weeks because it can damage neurotransmitters. One of the main reasons the DEA considers oxycodone a dangerous drug is the way your body develops **tolerance** to this drug class. According to the website www.drugabuse.gov, "drug tolerance typically develops because sending cells [in the neurons] reduce the amount of neurotransmitter they produce and release, or receiving cells withdraw receptors or otherwise dampen their responsiveness." When this happens, your brain needs higher amounts of the drug in order for it to function normally. This is what makes oxycodone and similar drugs addictive.

For example, one 5-milligram pill every four to six hours may modulate the pain for the first couple of weeks. Then you find you're still in pain taking that same amount, so

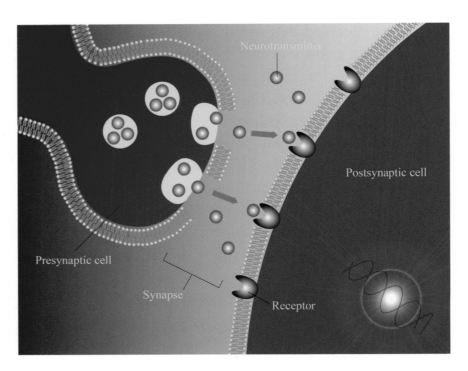

Neurotransmitters carry signals between neurons until they reach our brains. Drugs affect the function of neurons.

your doctor increases your dose to 10 milligrams every four to six hours. One of the side effects of oxycodone is that it slows your breathing, so a higher dose means a higher risk of **respiratory** failure.

"Some of my patients have become addicted because they had a skiing accident or a dental extraction, something very innocent, but were prescribed oxycodone and ended up developing some tolerance to it, needing more and more for the same desired effect, and then it got to the point where

they couldn't live without the drug," said Dr. Reef Karim, an addiction specialist and founder of The Control Center in Los Angeles. "They started abusing it, taking more of it, getting it in black market ways, tricking doctors, and it became a problem."

Early on, if you're using the drug illegally, you'll be seeking out more of it to achieve those same euphoric feelings from the first time. Over time, it won't just be the nice feelings a drug user will be craving. Oxycodone and other drugs in the opioid class are known to create physical dependence. This means it's not just that you *want* more of the drug, but that your body *needs* the drug to feel normal. Without the drug, you may experience withdrawal symptoms. Early symptoms of withdrawal may include agitation, anxiety, muscle aches, increased tearing, insomnia or having difficulty sleeping, runny nose, sweating, or excessive yawning. Later withdrawal symptoms have been described as: abdominal pain, diarrhea, dilated pupils, goose bumps, bone pain, or nausea and vomiting. At more mild levels, withdrawal may feel like the flu. At more severe levels, a person may feel violently ill, have difficulty getting out of bed, and vomit so much as to become dehydrated.

## A Look at OxyContin

In 1995, the US Food and Drug Administration (FDA) approved the use of OxyContin, which is the brand name for a drug with oxycodone. Scientists were able to introduce a time-release element to the drug, which made the government

# WINONA RYDER

Winona Ryder's life was spiraling downward when she was caught shoplifting while possessing oxycodone. The star of movies such as *Girl Interrupted* and *Little Women* said her road to abusing oxycodone began the way many people's do: with a prescription.

Ryder explained to *People* magazine that two months prior to her arrest she broke her arm, which naturally led to a trip to the doctor.

Winona Ryder is proof that money and fame won't save someone from forming an addiction.

"The doctor, a sort of quack doctor, was giving me a lot of stuff, and I was taking it at first to get through the pain," she told *People*. "And then there was this weird point when you don't know if you are in pain but you're taking it."

Money and fame does not make a person immune to making bad decisions with drugs. The addictive nature of oxycodone can hook anyone. And many won't stop until they face severe consequences.

Ryder later said that her being arrested "in a very weird way, was a blessing, because I couldn't do that [painkillers] anymore."

more interested in making it more widely available. This new element changed two things: it increased the amount of oxycodone in each pill and the amount of time before another dose was needed.

Prior to this development, all of the oxycodone in a pill would be released immediately inside of patients. With people feeling the full effects right away, they could safely withstand enough of the drug to last only four to six hours. In OxyContin, some of the drug is coated so it is not activated right away. This way, patients have less of the drug active in their system despite the fact the pill contains enough oxycodone to kill their pain for twelve hours.

Doctors decided that taking a pill every twelve hours instead of every four to six hours and having less of the drug active in a person's system would be safer for patients. It would also help them manage their pain. When used appropriately, OxyContin has done that. But it has also contributed to the skyrocketing number of overdoses.

Too many people took more OxyContin pills than their doctor recommended, they took them in ways that were not intended, or they took someone else's prescription.

When an OxyContin pill is crushed, the coating on the drug inside is broken. Warnings placed on bottles said: "OxyContin tablets are to be swallowed whole, and are not to be broken, chewed, or crushed. Swallowing broken, chewed, or crushed OxyContin tablets could lead to the rapid release and absorption of a potentially toxic dose of oxycodone," according to the CDC. The FDA has hypothesized that warning against crushing the pills may have alerted abusers to a method for misusing the drugs instead of educating potential abusers.

Swallowing, chewing, and crushing are not just different ways of getting the same drugs into your body. The effects of a medication or drug are always based on getting the chemicals from those drugs to the brain, which is when your body starts feeling the effects. These various routes of administering the drug impact the length of time it takes the chemicals to reach the brain. If you take the drug by mouth, the drug travels throughout most of your body, from your esophagus to your stomach and small intestine, where

Inhaling crushed oxycodone pills can be very dangerous.

they are absorbed into the bloodstream and head for the brain. This process can take several minutes.

If you're crushing the pills and snorting them through your nose, the drugs go straight from your nasal passage to the blood stream, and right to the brain. Some drug abusers may even crush the pills and dissolve them in water, so they can inject them. The effects then may be felt within seconds.

## Too Much Too Soon

Let's say you've suffered a terrible accident and are having extreme back pain, so your doctor prescribes a 20-milligram tablet of OxyContin that you are supposed to take every twelve hours. Give or take, that means your body is getting about 1.67 milligrams of the oxycodone each hour. If you crush it, dissolve it, and shoot it right into your arm, that's 20 milligrams that goes to your brain in a matter of seconds. This can be dangerous.

Fortunately, OxyContin was reformulated in 2010 to make the pills harder to crush and, hopefully, less likely and able to be abused. Purdue Pharma, the company that markets and distributes OxyContin, found that even when a user attempted to crush the new version of the pill, there were still larger pieces, which meant the drug wasn't getting absorbed as quickly. Studies have found that injecting OxyContin has become extremely difficult, if not impossible. Under the new formulation, the drug becomes gummy when mixed with water. Time will tell if these steps effectively cut down on the abuse of this drug class.

# CHAPTER THREE

# Gateway Drug

**T**HE EXPERIENCES CHILDREN HAVE WHEN using oxycodone are almost always detrimental. National Public Radio asked high schoolers who had used OxyContin about their experiences. One teenager, Ryan, talked about his downward spiral into addiction. He began using when he was sixteen. A week into trying to "have fun" with the drugs, Ryan realized if he didn't get a pill every day or two he started to get sick. He tried to kick the habit and started experiencing withdrawal symptoms. This is a very typical experience for someone who has become physically dependent on the drug.

"It was like somebody was inside of your head with a hammer," Ryan told NPR. "You feel like you're going to die. Just lying there in the bed, sweat pouring off of you

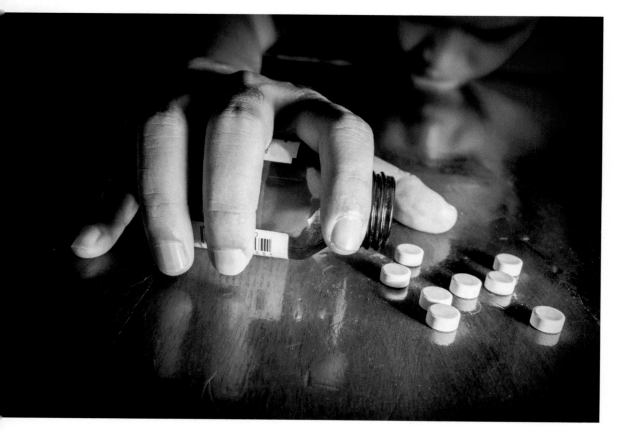

Addicted teenagers may find they have to take oxycodone to avoid feeling sick.

… Then five minutes later, you're freezing … then you'd be throwing up. I was sick as a dog and I was in bed and I couldn't believe it. I was actually scared."

Prescription drugs are the second-most misused drugs among teenagers, following marijuana. In 2013, 7.3 percent of twelve- to seventeen-year-olds reported abusing pain

relievers in their lifetime, and 20.8 percent of eighteen- to twenty-five-year-olds said they had used pain relievers without a prescription, according to the National Institute of Drug Abuse.

The journey to oxycodone addiction can be tumultuous. But authorities are learning right now that for many users, the drug abuse does not stop there. Pain reliever abuse is slowly declining, as the FDA has cracked down on prescription drugs, and OxyContin has reformulated its pills. Instead, use of a new drug is on the rise: heroin.

## From Oxy to Heroin

The reason many people transition from the oxycodone family (OxyContin or Percocet) to heroin is because both drugs are in the opioid family, meaning the same type of "high" is experienced with both. And, the prescription pills are more expensive than heroin. An 80-milligram oxycodone pill may sell for up to $92 on the streets, whereas a tiny balloon filled with a dose of heroin may cost $9, according to the director of substance abuse services in Charlotte, North Carolina. An average heroin user may take ten or more doses per day.

DEA Special Agent Amy Roderick told *USA Today*, "Once you're addicted to an opiate, you're addicted. If you can't get what you want, you'll take what you can get."

A middle-class, suburban mom from Massachusetts recalled the hold drugs took on her son, Christopher. His drug abuse began with Percocet, which a doctor had prescribed to him following a football injury. This led to him and his

Heroin is cheaper than oxycodone, so its use is on the rise.

friends experimenting with OxyContin. They got hooked, and within the next year, her son was using heroin.

Christopher does not project the image of a "bad" kid. His mom said he was the captain of the football and wrestling teams and was popular among his teammates. He got good grades and was never in trouble at school. "He was the

kind of kid who would walk through the mall with me and hold my hand," his mom told NPR. "He didn't care what other people thought and said. Christopher was just his own person." But the drug took hold. Christopher died of a heroin overdose at age nineteen.

The number of heroin users in the United States has nearly doubled in the past six years, from 373,000 in 2007 to 681,000 in 2013, according to SAMHSA. In 2013, 169,000 people used heroin for the first time. In New Jersey alone, 741 people died from a heroin overdose in 2013.

"We're seeing it more and more," said Robert Budsock, the CEO of Integrity House, a treatment program in New Jersey. "They are quickly moving from prescription drugs to heroin. It's like lightning. Heroin now is easier to get. The big risk is at least with prescription drugs you know they're FDA-approved. You don't have that with heroin, and that's why it's so easy to overdose."

Drug users who transition from oxycodone to heroin are also more likely to administer their drugs by injection. This leads to increased risk for long-term health problems. If a person is trying to inject oxycodone, that means he or she is crushing the pills and trying to dissolve them in water. However, the tablet will not dissolve completely, even if it looks like it has. Over time, tiny particles of the tablet will build up in the bloodstream and could lead to blocked veins and kidney problems. Continuing to inject drugs in the same area also can cause damage to the skin and veins, leading to abscesses or collapsed veins. Desperate addicts have been

# Temporary Relief

You must realize by now that overdosing from illegally using oxycodone is a big possibility. The drug slows down your central nervous system, and it can slow your breathing to deadly rates.

To combat overdoses, more police officers are being equipped with Narcan, which is the trade name for naloxone. Narcan is an **antidote** that can temporarily reverse the effects of an overdose on heroin, codeine, fentanyl, hydrocodone, hydromorphone, methadone, morphine, and oxycodone, all drugs in the opioid family. Narcan can be injected or administered similar to a nasal spray.

Some police stations are offering free Narcan training to citizens. One county in New Jersey has distributed 250 Narcan Kits to its police officers.

"Equipping our officers with these Narcan Kits will enable them to take immediate life-saving measures even prior to the arrival of Emergency Medical Services personnel," Montclair town police chief Todd Conforti said.

A harm-reduction nurse in New Mexico demonstrates how to use Narcan nasal spray.

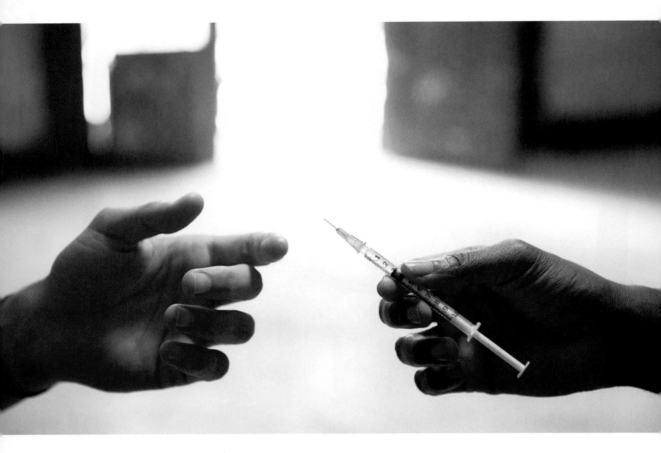

Sharing needles is a dangerous habit among drug users that can lead to the spread of life-threatening diseases.

known to try to inject the drugs in their femoral vein in the groin area, which is particularly dangerous because of the medical complications that may arise.

Finally, there are extreme risks of infection for needle users, who may contract HIV or hepatitis when using shared or **non-sterile**, unclean injection equipment. HIV, which

stands for the Human Immunodeficiency Virus, is a life-threatening infection to the body's immune system that can cause AIDS. Hepatitis C, the most common form of hepatitis among needle users, is a contagious liver disease that can develop into a serious, lifelong illness.

Rates of three forms of hepatitis, psychiatric illnesses, and pancreatitis were up to thirty-six times higher in prescription drug users than in people who aren't abusers.

## HEALTH PROBLEMS

Even if an oxycodone user doesn't progress to injecting drugs with a needle or using heroin, there are several health risks. Those who use opioids experienced higher rates of cardiovascular (heart) problems and had more bone fractures, according to a study by the Archives of Internal Medicine. Oxycodone abusers also may have noticeably bloodshot eyes, flushed skin, or small pupils. Significant changes in weight, usually extreme drops, may occur due to changes in eating habits.

Acute health risks may include nausea, vomiting, dry mouth, sweating, itching, fatigue, headaches, or dizziness. More severe risks can affect your life at home and at school or work, and may include shortness of breath, shallow breathing, cold and clammy skin, a slowed pulse, confusion, passing out, or seizures.

Over the long run, an oxycodone user may experience liver or kidney problems. These two organs are instrumental in processing the **toxins** in your body, so if your liver and kidneys are forced to work overtime to clear your system from regular or long-term oxycodone use, they may begin to fail.

Many oxycodone abusers find they entirely neglect personal hygiene. When a person is chasing a high or losing a battle with addiction, nothing is as important as taking more of the drug. One former user shared this part of her story with her treatment center:

"Over the course of several weeks, I stopped showering or brushing my teeth, and I slept in my clothes. The house looked as if a tornado had hit it, with stacks of dirty dishes in the sink and laundry piled up. I stopped answering the phone altogether. I had no appetite and felt sick afterward when I did eat. I kept telling myself that I would stop tomorrow, but it was obvious, even to me, that I had lost the ability to make a conscious choice.

"As the months went by, my overall health and appearance dramatically declined. I had lost almost forty pounds, and there were dark circles under my eyes. My hair was a disheveled mess, and my body odor was pungent. At times I would go weeks without taking a shower."

Almost fifteen thousand people died from oxycodone overdoses in 2008. Three main symptoms indicate an oxycodone overdose: extreme sleepiness, breathing problems, and small pupils (the black circle in the colored part of your eye). Depending on how much of the drug has been taken, a person may have difficulty staying awake or may become completely unconscious.

Drug users may find they neglect basic tasks like showering because using the drug has become their only priority.

Patients or drug abusers face another risk when they mix oxycodone or other painkillers with alcohol. "These painkillers are particularly dangerous because they depress the central nervous system, slowing down breathing and the brain stem's responsiveness to carbon dioxide to the point where someone abusing these medications can simply stop breathing," warns Dr. Sanjay Gupta, a well-known neurosurgeon who often appears on TV. "Combine these painkillers with alcohol, another depressant, and you've got a recipe for disaster."

Basically, Dr. Gupta is pointing out that along with their benefits, painkillers also slow down your breathing. Alcohol has the same effect on the body, so a combination of the two could shut down your respiratory system. Oxycodone is nothing to play around with.

# CHAPTER FOUR

# Paying the Price

**T**HE HEALTH RISKS OF CONTINUED oxycodone use are extreme, but abuse of this painkiller can be detrimental to many other areas of your life. The oxycodone drug class is highly addictive. This means once you get hooked, you just want more and more and more to feel the same high—and then just to feel normal.

Think about it this way: what began as something to kill pain or have fun begins controlling your life. But at this point you've spent weeks waking up and taking a pill every morning, so you keep doing it. You can't function without them.

The inordinate amount of time it takes to find and take all these oxycodone pills doesn't leave you much time for anything else. But it's more than just the time. Think about all the other problems that could come with needing to seek out these drugs over and over again.

First, look at the money required. When legally sold, a 10-milligram tablet of OxyContin will cost about $1.25, and an 80-milligram tablet will cost about $6. But on the streets where pills are sold and bought illegally, they are way more expensive. The DEA found in 2009 the average street price for OxyContin is $1.15 per milligram. That means about $11.50 for a 10-milligram pill and about $92 for an 80-milligram pill. One night of experimenting with drugs could cost as much as many older teens earn in a week in a part-time job.

When people develop an addiction, their body will crave more of the drug. If they don't give it what it needs, they will start experiencing withdrawal symptoms. That $92 as a one-time experiment may turn into a habit requiring one or more pills every day. Addicts in the early stages need hundreds of dollars a week to sustain their habits. Most children and teenagers don't have this kind of cash, so what do they do? The most commonly reported ways of obtaining money are: stealing from friends or family members, shoplifting, and prostitution. Someone thinking, "Well, I would never do any of those things," has the same mind-set of most people who think they're just having fun with a drug. It's once they're addicted that they find they will do almost anything to get the money for their next fix.

Ryan, the teenager interviewed by NPR, said first it was his own cash that disappeared because of his OxyContin addiction. Ryan says he cashed in $7,000 in savings bonds his aunts had given him for birthdays in years past. He sold his

40

Some teens resort to stealing money from their families to support their drug habit.

PlayStation, leather jackets, cell phone—basically, everything he had—just to stay high and keep from getting sick. Katie, an eighteen-year-old who was recovering from an OxyContin addiction at the time of her interview, remembers taking advantage of her parents. Katie stole her parents' ATM card and took $5,000 out of their account. She stole her mother's checkbooks and wrote checks, forging her mother's name. She stole cameras and jewelry and even her father's wedding

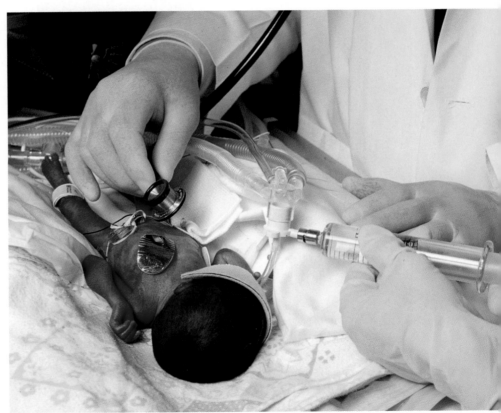

If a woman uses opioid drugs while pregnant, her baby probably will be born addicted to the drugs.

ring; then she sold everything to have money to pay for her pills. Nothing mattered more than getting more drugs.

Promiscuous behavior and prescription drug abuse present another problem. Pregnant women can pass on an addiction to their unborn babies. Opioids cause withdrawal symptoms that are among the worst, and 55 to 90 percent of babies born to an opioid addict will go through withdrawal.

Some people who thought the money was too hard to come by stole the pills themselves. One man who worked for a pharmacy in Long Island was discovered to have stolen 5,600 pills from the hospital that employed him. Needless to say, he suffered legal consequences.

Trying to come up with hundreds of dollars a week proves to be an insurmountable challenge for many oxycodone users. This is why many oxycodone abusers often turn to heroin, despite the fact that it's an illegal drug. Remember, though, over time a person will need more and more heroin, just like he or she would need more and more pills.

Why is heroin so much cheaper? First of all, there is a huge supply of opium poppies, largely centered in Afghanistan, with other pockets in Central Europe and South America. These poppies are used to create heroin. Also, the Federal Drug Administration does not oversee or regulate heroin, so heroin sellers may mix the pure stuff with cheaper drugs or even baby powder and charge drug users the same price.

After OxyContin was reformulated in 2010 to make it harder to crush, abusers had a lot more difficulty snorting or injecting the drug. This helped cut down on the rates of OxyContin abuse—from 2010 to 2012, the choice of

OxyContin as a drug of abuse went from 35.6 percent to 12.8 percent among opioid abusers. The bad news? Sixty-six percent of former OxyContin users reported they had switched to heroin. Among those who made the transition was the late Philip Seymour Hoffman, a Hollywood actor who died of an overdose.

The cost in money and lives to society of the prescription drug abuse epidemic is huge. Oxycodone is a depressant and can affect a person's driving. The National Highway Transportation Safety Administration said that eighteen percent of fatally injured drivers tested positive for at least one prescription drug in 2009, up from 13 percent in 2005. More than 16 percent of nighttime and weekend drivers were found to be under the influence of legal and illegal drugs.

Prescription opioid abuse in the United States in 2007 cost society an estimated $55.7 billion. The costs were divided into three areas: workplace costs ($25.6 billion), health care costs ($25 billion), and criminal justice costs ($5.1 billion). Contributing to workplace costs were earnings lost due to premature death, time lost to illness, or the loss of a job. Health care costs consisted primarily of excess medical and prescription costs. Criminal justice costs were largely composed of correctional facility and police costs.

This doesn't take into account the cost to insurance companies. Addicts commonly employ what is known as drug diversion, which is using drugs that have a medical purpose for recreation. To support this practice, they go doctor shopping.

# THE COST OF A HABIT

This isn't math class, but one treatment center helps us break down the dollars and cents of trying to maintain an OxyContin addiction. The Novus Medical Detox Center in Florida took a look at the people facing addiction who came to their treatment center. They found people who were addicted to OxyContin were using 80 to 400 milligrams per day.

The DEA found the average cost is $1.15 per milligram, so here are the calculations: Let's assume a person is using about 120 milligrams a day, which is on the lower side but more likely for an addict in the earlier stages. This would mean $138 each day and $4,140 for each month. And an OxyContin addict who maintains that dose for a whole year would find him or herself spending $49,680. That's an awful lot of money to scrounge together for a drug that is slowly—or quickly—destroying your life.

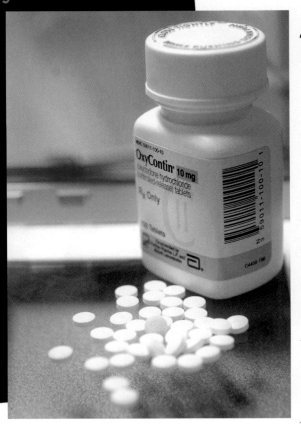

One pill bottle can turn into a lot of wasted money for an OxyContin addict.

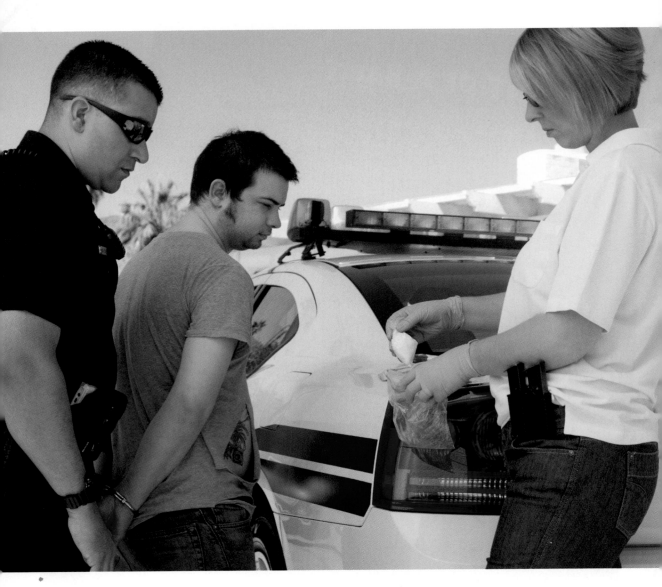

Using prescription drugs without a prescription is illegal and can lead to many bad consequences.

Someone who is doctor shopping tries to get treatment from several doctors at the same time for the same problem, thereby getting each doctor to write a drug prescription. This leads to insurance fraud, which is the main source of money for drug diversion. Fraud costs health insurance companies more than $70 billion every year.

Stealing, prostitution, heroin, and death by overdose are extreme outcomes of an oxycodone addiction. There is another factor to consider: the law. Every state has its own laws regarding the consequences of being caught with OxyContin or other prescription painkillers without a prescription. In Florida, possession of just seven prescription pain pills for which you do not have a prescription qualifies as drug trafficking and comes with a mandatory minimum prison sentence of three years. There's a fair chance almost any OxyContin addict could be caught with that amount of pills in his possession—some users need that many pills just to get out of bed in the morning.

Former drug addicts have shared their stories about all they've lost. If you're thinking you'll have time for—or care about—going to soccer practice, school dances, the movies, family reunions, or even your own birthday party, you're probably wrong. For an abuser, drugs are all that matter.

## CHAPTER FIVE

# Get Some Help

IN 2006, PHILIP SEYMOUR HOFFMAN predicted that if he had not sought rehab for his multiple drug addictions, he would have been dead. At that time, when he was recalling his drug use trajectory on CBS, the Oscar-winning actor known for his roles in *The Hunger Games: Catching Fire* and *Capote* had been **sober** for sixteen years.

"It was all that [drugs and alcohol], yeah, it was anything I could get my hands on," Hoffman told CBS reporter Steve Kroft. "I liked it all.

"I went [to rehab]. I got sober when I was twenty-two years old. You get panicked … and I got panicked for my life. It was really just that. I have so much empathy for these young actors that are nineteen and all of a sudden they're beautiful and famous and rich. I'm like, 'Oh my God. I'd be dead.'"

Philip Seymour Hoffman's death put a public face on the tragic outcomes that can come from opioid use.

Hoffman understood the dangers of staying addicted and living a drug-filled lifestyle. He remained sober for many years. Unfortunately, Hoffman suffered a **relapse**, and his return to drugs ultimately led to his death at age forty-six. Relapses occur for drug users because of the long-term impact drug use has on a person's brain. Even if the rational part of your mind knows the drugs are no good for you, there is still a part of your brain that remains addicted, even after years of sobriety.

While Hoffman's untimely death was devastating to many of his fans, it also serves as a warning to many wrapped up in the throes of addiction: treatment is necessary.

In 2009, 23.5 million people in the United States needed treatment for their abuse of alcohol or **illicit** drugs. Of them, 20 percent—or 4.7 million people—needed treatment for opioids, including oxycodone, heroin or other painkillers.

## Getting Off Slowly

Why do people need treatment? Why can't they *just stop*? The withdrawal symptoms from oxycodone can be incredibly difficult to deal with—from vomiting and diarrhea to cold flashes and insomnia. Once your body has developed a tolerance to a drug, your body adapts and then comes to expect it. When you try to give up the drug, your body goes through a period of readjustment. Your body doesn't really remember what it was like to be without the drug! Repeated drug use also causes changes to take place in your brain. The parts of your brain needed to learn and remember, make

good decisions, and control your impulses are impaired by continued drug use. This means you're trying to make a really tough change with somewhat faulty equipment.

A person cannot actually die from stopping oxycodone **cold turkey,** or abruptly giving it up all at once. While unpleasant, the withdrawal symptoms will eventually go away. However, it may be determined that it is safer to **detox** from the drug in a treatment center, where medical professionals will supervise your symptoms and help you manage the physical and mental pain of being without the drug.

How do you know if you have a problem, and what should you do about seeking treatment? Step one: ask for help!

First, you should share your concerns with a parent or trusted adult. Then, you should look into scheduling an appointment with a doctor. A doctor will typically ask a series of questions about your drug use, perhaps looking for information about how much you have used, how often, and for how long. He or she may also ask if you have been involved in risky behaviors like driving under the influence or having unprotected sex. We know this might sound uncomfortable, but it's important to remember that nothing is more important than your life—and all these answers will get you one step closer to saving it. As always, honesty is the best policy.

It's likely that some sort of treatment will follow, but this may come in many forms. The longer you have been using oxycodone, the more likely it is that treatment in a detox center will be necessary, to help flush your system of

# Warning Signs of Oxycodone Abuse

Physical signs you may experience yourself or observe or hear about from your friends:

- Drowsiness, sometimes to the point of falling asleep
- Sedation, or extremely calm state
- Euphoria, a state of intense happiness or self-confidence
- Lightheadedness
- Itching
- Nausea and vomiting
- Constipation
- Low blood pressure
- Respiratory suppression or trouble breathing
- Headache
- Dry mouth
- Sweating
- Constricted pupils

Behavioral signs you may experience yourself or observe or hear about from your friends:

- Hanging out with different friends
- Not caring about your appearance
- Getting worse grades
- Missing classes or skipping school
- Losing interest in your favorite activities
- Getting in trouble in school or with the law
- Having different eating or sleeping habits
- Having more problems with family members and friends

Drug users who have become accustomed to high doses of oxycodone have been known to have trouble staying awake.

Treatment programs may be an important part of a person's journey to recovery and sobriety.

the drug in a safe environment. If you're still early in the addiction and a doctor thinks you can handle the withdrawal symptoms at home, you may be an appropriate candidate for **outpatient** treatment. This may be set up in several ways, but many programs require you to commit to an hour or so in the evenings, so you can still attend school during the day. Methadone maintenance is a treatment method mostly used for adults. Methadone is a drug in the opioid family, but used in appropriate doses administered by a doctor or treatment agency, it can help a person avoid withdrawal symptoms without getting them high. Methadone replaces the oxycodone in a safer way, though it is still a drug.

Methadone can help someone escape drugs. However, there are reasons why young people use drugs to try to escape. Kyle Keegan wrote about his journey into addiction, which started around age twelve with alcohol and marijuana. He eventually took every drug in the book, from Percocet to heroin. He offers insight to any child or teenager who is thinking about drug experimentation in his book, *Chasing the High*.

"At some point in my childhood I began to feel great pressure to fit in with the other kids, pressure to be cool, to be accepted by others," he wrote. "These feelings opened a gap that would slowly distance me from my family. By the time I was around eight or nine years old I began to think I was not as strong or as fast or even as smart as most of my friends. I felt that I was often the butt of practical jokes. Fitting in became everything to me, and being accepted by the other kids was the ultimate achievement. I couldn't shake the feeling that I somehow just didn't belong. I could not stand to be myself and eventually learned to escape these bad feelings by altering my state of mind with foreign substances."

After years of fighting his addiction, Keegan had an epiphany about his drug use.

"I soon realized that I had never truly accepted myself for who I was," he wrote. "In time, I developed a relationship with myself and figured out that the more my self-esteem grew and the more I learned to love myself, the less need I would have for the drugs I had used to mask my feelings, emotions, and even my identity."

Finally, you may want to explore Teen Narcotics Anonymous meetings, where you can meet other teens, like Keegan, in **recovery** from their addictions. They may share your feelings and be able to identify with the difficulty of resuming a drug-free life.

## Change Habits

Recovering from oxycodone abuse may also require some lifestyle changes. Addicts in recovery are often told to avoid the people, places, and things that they associate with their addiction. If your friends were abusing the drug with you, you may have to consider a different social circle. If the bleachers after school were where you used to get high, you may want to consider avoiding that area during after-school hours. Going to parties where alcohol is present may also be

Who you choose to hang out with may greatly affect your odds of experimenting with drugs or recovering from an addiction to them.

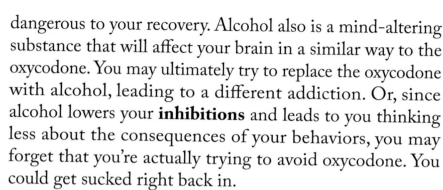

dangerous to your recovery. Alcohol also is a mind-altering substance that will affect your brain in a similar way to the oxycodone. You may ultimately try to replace the oxycodone with alcohol, leading to a different addiction. Or, since alcohol lowers your **inhibitions** and leads to you thinking less about the consequences of your behaviors, you may forget that you're actually trying to avoid oxycodone. You could get sucked right back in.

The changes necessary to be successful in recovery aren't meant to scare you. The main message is this: The easiest way to never have to beat an addiction is to never get one started. But if you do find yourself addicted to oxycodone, it's important to remember that the drug does not need to rule the rest of your life. Treatment is available. Sharing your difficulties with a parent, teacher, coach, or doctor may be the first step in conquering your addiction and saving your life.

# Glossary

**antidote** A medicine or remedy that counteracts the effect of a poison or disease.

**cold turkey** Abrupt and complete withdrawal from the use of an addictive substance.

**detox** Medical treatment to help a person gradually overcome an addiction.

**epidemic** A widespread occurrence of a disease or problem in an area.

**heroin** A narcotic powder refined from morphine that is highly addictive.

**hydrocodone** A semi-synthetic opioid drug derived from codeine and thebaine.

**illicit** Something that is unlawful, or forbidden by rules or custom.

**inhibition** The ability to hold back or show restraint from doing something.

**methadone** A synthetic opiate used as a heroin substitute and in drug treatment programs.

**narcotic** A class of substances that blunt the senses and can cause addiction.

**non-sterile** Not clean or free from exposure to germs.

**opioid** A group of synthetic substances that affect how a body responds to stress and pain.

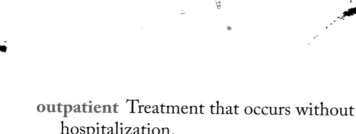

**outpatient** Treatment that occurs without hospitalization.

**receptors** A region of tissue or a molecule in a cell membrane that responds to a particular neurotransmitter, hormone, or other substance.

**recovery** A process of restoring one's health in overcoming an addiction.

**relapse** The return of an illness or to fall back into former practices, such as drug-using.

**respiratory** The system responsible for breathing.

**sober** Not intoxicated or drunk; or for an addict, not using a drug.

**tolerance** The reduced reaction to a drug, so that more of it is needed to produce the same results.

**toxicology** The science of dealing with the effects of drugs or poisons.

**toxins** Poisons produced by an organism.

**withdrawal** May occur if someone attempts to stop taking a drug. Symptoms of withdrawal include seizures, psychosis, severe insomnia, and severe anxiety.

# Find Out More

## Books

Bjornlund, Lydia. *Oxycodone.* Compact Research Series. San Diego, CA: Referencepoint Press, 2011.

Lew, Kristi. *The Truth About Oxycodone and Other Narcotics.* Drugs and Consequences. New York: Rosen Publishing Group, 2014.

Lockwood, Brad. *OxyContin: From Pain Relief to Addiction.* Drug Abuse & Society: Cost to a Nation. New York: Rosen Publishing Group, 2006.

Petersen, Christine. *Vicodin and OxyContin.* Dangerous Drugs. New York: Cavendish Square Publishing, 2013.

Pinsky, Drew, Marvin D. Seppala, Robert J. Meyers, John Gardin, and William White. *When Painkillers Become Dangerous: What Everyone Needs to Know About OxyContin and Other Prescription Drugs.* Center City, MN: Hazelden, 2004.

# Websites

**Connecticut Department of Consumer Protection**
www.ct.gov/dcp/lib/dcp/drug_control/pmp/
pdf/oxycodone.pdf

Read or download a copy of "Oxycodone: Protect Your Teens," an informational pamphlet for parents of teens.

**National Institute on Drug Abuse (NIDA)**
www.drugabuse.gov

In addition to information on drug abuse for people of all ages, check out the Teens section for an easy-to-read guide that will help you determine if your drug use may have become a problem.

**Project Know: Teen OxyContin Abuse**
www.projectknow.com/research/teen-oxycontin-addiction

This is an article for teens and parents to assist them in understanding teen OxyContin use.

**Teen Drug Abuse**
www.teen-drug-abuse.org

This site provides information on teen drug use, describes drugs such as oxycodone and their effects, and gives guidance on how you can help yourself or someone else get treatment.

# Index

Page numbers in **boldface** are illustrations. Entries in **boldface** are glossary terms.

## About the Author

**Jackie F. Stanmyre** is a former award-winning journalist at the *Star-Ledger* of Newark, New Jersey. She currently works as a mental health and addiction counselor. She lives in Montclair, New Jersey, with her husband and their two cats.